1743 Th Jefferson 1826

from the original portrait by Gilbert Stuart in possession
of Bowdoin College~Brunswick, Maine

JEFFERSON THE MAN

In His Own Words

Edited by Robert C. Baron

Fulcrum/Starwood Publishing
in association with the Library of Congress
Golden, Colorado, and Washington, D.C.

Library of Congress Cataloging-in-Publication Data

Jefferson, the man : in his own words / edited by Robert C. Baron in
   association with the Library of Congress.
            p.   cm.
   Includes bibliographical references.
   ISBN 1-56373-025-1
      1. Jefferson, Thomas, 1743–1826—Quotations. I. Jefferson,
   Thomas, 1743–1826. II. Baron, Robert C. III. Library of Congress.
   E302.J442   1993
   973.4'6'092—dc20   92-45121
                                                                  CIP

Printed in the United States of America

0   9   8   7   6   5   4   3   2   1

Fulcrum/Starwood Publishing
350 Indiana Street, Suite 350
Golden, Colorado 80401–5093

CONTENTS

THE LEGACY OF
THOMAS JEFFERSON

Thomas Jefferson was born April 13, 1743, at Shadwell, Goochland (now Albermarle) County, Virginia, the first son of Peter Jefferson and Jane Randolph Jefferson. Educated at the College of William and Mary, he studied law and mathematics. His public service was extensive: a member of the Virginia House of Burgess, representative to the Second Continental Congress, governor of Virginia, diplomat, minister to France, secretary of state under President Washington, vice president under John Adams, and two term president of the United States (1801–1809).

The private man may even be more interesting than the public one. Jefferson's personal life was difficult. His father died when Jefferson was 14; his mother died when he was 32. When Jefferson's wife died at the age of 33, after they had been married less than ten years, Jefferson's grief knew no bounds. Of their six children, four died in infancy, and his daughter Mary died at age 26, while Jefferson was president. Only his oldest daughter, Martha, outlived him. Yet, Jefferson somehow managed to rise above the personal tragedies and accomplish much, both as a public and a private man. The adjectives optimistic, tolerant, and serene have been applied to him.

This is a book about Thomas Jefferson, in his own words. Jefferson was a multitalented man—a farmer, gardener, scientist, inventor, lawyer, humanist, scholar, writer, philosopher, architect, art collector, musician, educator, neighbor, parent, and grandparent.

As we celebrate the 250th anniversary of Jefferson's birth, in April 1993, it is perhaps a time for reflection. While other heroes of the American Revolution have faded in the American memory, while others have remained figures of their own time and place, Jefferson continues to stand out not only as one of the great figures of his era, but as an inspiration today as democracies continue to form and new challenges to democratic self-government are faced. If one were to make a list of the most important world figures over the last three centuries, Jefferson's name would be near the top of the list. Indeed, with time, Jefferson's name and image have gotten brighter. Why?

Around 1800, Jefferson wrote a memorandum on services to his country.

> I have sometimes asked myself whether my country is the better for my having lived at all? I do not know that it is. I have been the instrument of doing the following things; but they would have been done by others; some of them, perhaps, a little better.

Jefferson then listed a number of accomplishments including:

- Clearing the Rivanna River
- The Declaration of Independence
- Demolition of the church establishment and legalizing freedom of religion
- Freedom to move anywhere with one's family
- The act prohibiting the import of slaves
- Prison reform
- Importing olive plants and upland rice to South Carolina
- Establishment of public schools

This memorandum shows the breadth of the man as well as his humility. Two decades later, Thomas Jefferson requested for his tombstone "the following inscription, & not one word more":

> Here was Buried
> Thomas Jefferson
> Author of the Declaration of American Independence
> of the Statute of Virginia for religious freedom
> and Father of the University of Virginia.

"because by these, as testimonials that I have lived, I wish most to be remembered."

On July 4, 1826, Thomas Jefferson, an old man at 83 but still a young gardener and student, died at his beloved Monticello. On that same day, the fiftieth anniversary of the Declaration of Independence, John Adams, his old friend and colleague, died in Massachusetts.

For a time, Jefferson's star faded. He was a southerner and a slave owner, and the country's views on these issues diminished Jefferson's image. Forgotten was the fact that he had spoken out against slavery, that the original draft of the Declaration of Independence blamed King George for suppressing every legislative attempt to prohibit slavery in the new world, that Jefferson had recommended legislation for the western territories forbidding slavery in all new states, and that as president he had forbidden the importation of slaves as soon as it was allowed by the Constitution.

After his death, Monticello was sold to pay debts. Few people were interested in Jefferson's personal papers. They were bequeathed to his grandson, Thomas Jefferson Randolph, and then collected by Jefferson's great-grandson, Thomas Jefferson Coolidge. Few were interested in Jefferson's ideas. The 1866 edition of *Bartlett's Famous Quotations* contains not one quote of Thomas Jefferson. Subsequent editions of *Bartlett's* began to acknowledge the wisdom of Jefferson, and by 1882, there were eight Jefferson quotes. The current issue of *Bartlett's* has fifty quotes by Jefferson, more than George Washington, James Madison, John Hancock, Richard Henry Lee, Robert Morris, Robert Treat Paine, George Mason, Alexander Hamilton, Sam Adams, and John Dickinson combined.

For over one hundred years, Jefferson's star has shown brighter and brighter. Where prior to the Civil War, he was vilified, today he shares the image of Washington as being considered almost a god and not a man. But he was a man, even if a very special man. A reading of his words in this book, as well as a reading of the biographies listed in the Bibliography, shows what an exceptional man Jefferson was.

Thomas Jefferson was a very versatile man. His thoughts on America, democracy, independence, exploration, science, gardening, education, books, religion, and friends and family show his breadth. In April 1962, President John F. Kennedy hosted a dinner for Nobel Prize winners of the Western Hemisphere and said: "I think this is the most extraordinary collection of talent, of human knowledge, that has been ever gathered together at the White House, with the possible exception of when Thomas Jefferson dined alone."

Jefferson reminds us that at a time of increasing specialization and one-dimensional leaders, it is possible for a human to study in many fields and become knowledgeable in several. Our capabilities are much deeper than we allow, and we all become better by trying to follow in Jefferson's footsteps, by studying and recognizing that education is a continuous process.

Jefferson was an optimist. He wrote Adams: "I like the dreams of the future more than the history of the past." He believed that things could get better, that we in America are the hope of all mankind. In general, we as Americans are an optimistic people, believing that America is a very special place and that life will be ever better for our children.

Jefferson was a farmer and gardener who believed that agriculture was the strength of our country. Americans are a people of the land. As we have grown from a population of 3 million in 1790 to 250 million two centuries later, it is important to realize that this was possible because we have been able to feed our people. Agriculture has been and is the foundation of any country. Its importance continues to be shown in the Soviet Union, Africa, Asia, and throughout the world.

Jefferson believed in the American West. He "stretched the Constitution until it cracked" in order to purchase Louisiana, doubling the size of the country and changing America from an Atlantic seaboard nation to one that spanned the continent. He sent Lewis and Clark west to explore the country and gave them specific instructions on what to see and record. For over sixty years, every explorer followed the directions of Jefferson, and the country, slowly but surely, followed Jefferson's vision west, not east toward Europe.

One of the founders of this country and a lifelong fighter for liberty, Jefferson remained a revolutionary. He fought for freedom of opportunity, freedom of thought, free public schools and educational opportunity, a state library, freedom of religion, equal justice under the law, freedom to change jobs and move. He had a very specific view of the role of government as the servant and not the master of the people.

Jefferson believed in a continued fight for freedom and independence. Abraham Lincoln, in a letter dated April 6, 1858, wrote: "All honor to Jefferson, to the man who ... had the coolness, forecast, and capacity to introduce into a merely revolutionary document, an abstract truth ... that today, and in all coming days, shall be a rebuke to tyranny and rebellion."

And so we return to the original question. Why, with time, has Jefferson's name and image gotten brighter? Certainly a part of it is his accomplishments. But, in my view, it is more than what Jefferson did, it is also what he was, what he believed in, and how that affects each of us.

Because he was so broadly interested in so many things, Jefferson is a mirror that each of us can look into and see ourselves and our dreams. He has something of interest to everybody. Through him, we can see the best of America and what it can become.

Dumas Malone wrote a magnificent six-volume biography of Jefferson. He closed the last volume with these words:

> He [Jefferson] was limited by his own time and circumstances and he made concessions to the society in which he lived. But he perceived eternal values and supported timeless causes. Thus he became one of the most notable champions of freedom and enlightenment in recorded history.

A particular reflection of Jefferson's championship of enlightenment is the Library of Congress, America's oldest national cultural institution and our partner in presenting this collection of Jefferson's thoughts. The story of Jefferson's role as principal founder of the Library and his deep involvement in its evolution is outlined in John Y. Cole's introductory essay to this volume. Now the largest library in the world and a national and international resource of unparalleled dimensions, the Library of Congress holds Jefferson's presidential papers and his personal library, and expresses in the breadth and diversity of its collections his belief in knowledge as the cornerstone of democracy. *Thomas Jefferson the Man: In His Own Words* is one of a series of books based on Library of Congress collections that Fulcrum/ Starwood is publishing in association with the Library—which itself is very much a part of Jefferson's legacy to his nation and the world.

Now listen to the words of Thomas Jefferson.

—*Robert C. Baron,* Publisher

THOMAS JEFFERSON AND THE LIBRARY OF CONGRESS

The Library of Congress, America's oldest national cultural institution, was established in 1800 as the national legislature of the new Republic of the United States prepared to move from Philadelphia to the new capital city of Washington. In 1801, its collections consisted of 740 books and three maps. Today, it is the largest library in the world, occupying three buildings on Capitol Hill. Its collections include approximately fifteen million books, thirty-nine million manuscripts, thirteen million photographs, four million maps, more than three and a half million pieces of music, and more than half a million motion pictures. The Library's collection of more than fifty-six hundred incunabula (books printed before 1500) is the largest in the Western Hemisphere, and its collection of maps, atlases, newspapers, music, motion pictures, photographs, and microforms are probably the largest in the world. Approximately two thirds of the books in the Library's collections are in languages other than English. Its Chinese, Russian, Japanese, Korean, and Polish collections are the largest outside of those countries, and the Arabic collections are the largest outside of Egypt. Its collection of Luso-Hispanic materials is the largest in the world. The richness and diversity of its collections has made the Library a vital resource for Congress, the nation, and researchers from around the globe.

How did a library established by the legislature for its own use become such an ambitious and comprehensive institution? The ideals, intellectual curiosity, and pragmatism of Thomas Jefferson are the keys to this transformation.

Jefferson believed that the power of intellect could shape a free and democratic society. As a man who said he could not live without books, Jefferson took a keen interest in the Library of Congress and its collections while he was president of the United States from 1801 to 1809. On January 26, 1802, President

Jefferson approved the first law defining the role and functions of the new institution. Throughout Jefferson's presidency, he personally recommended books for the Library and appointed the first two librarians of Congress

In 1814, the British army invaded the city of Washington and burned the Capitol, including the three-thousand-volume Library of Congress. By then retired to Monticello, Jefferson offered to sell his personal library, the largest and finest in the country, to the Congress to "recommence" its library. Jefferson believed that the American national legislature needed ideas and information on all subjects and in many languages in order to govern a democracy. Anticipating the argument that his collection might be too comprehensive, he emphasized that there was "no subject to which a member of Congress might not have occasion to refer." The purchase of Jefferson's 6,487 volumes for $23,940 was approved in 1815. When the books arrived, the Library of Congress also adopted the classification system devised by Jefferson and continued to use it until the turn of the century.

The library that Jefferson sold to Congress not only included over twice the number of volumes that had been in the destroyed Library of Congress, it expanded the scope of the Library far beyond the bounds of a legislative library devoted primarily to legal, economic, and historical works. Jefferson was a man on encyclopedic interests; his library included works on architecture, the arts, science, literature, and geography. It contained books in French, Spanish, German, Latin, Greek, and one three-volume statistical work in Russian.

The acquisition by Congress of Jefferson's library was the basis for the expansion of the Library's functions, as well as its collections. Today, the Library of Congress brings together the diverse interests of government, scholarship, and librarianship. The Library reflects Jefferson's deep appreciation for the arts. His passionate devotion to music is found not only in the Music Division's collections, but in the classical and folk music concerts held at the Library and in the musical works the Library commissions (among the most famous is Aaron Copland's "Appalachian Spring"). Jefferson's love for books and literature is reflected in the programs of the Center for the Book and in the fact that the poet laureate of the United States is housed at the Library. The Jeffersonian concept of universiality is the principle that unifies these diverse endeavors.

In 1943, the Library commemorated the bicentennial of Jefferson's birth. In opening the Library's exhibit, then Librarian of Congress Archibald MacLeish called Jefferson's definition of liberty the "greatest and the most moving, as it is the most articulate." In 1993, the 250th anniversary of Jefferson's birth, the Library, under the leadership of Librarian of Congress James H. Billington, is drawing on its Jeffersonian legacy to launch a series of events and activities that will culminate in the Library's bicentennial year of 2000. These activities will demonstrate the importance of an open comprehensive national library to the successful functioning of a democratic, culturally diverse society. They will also demonstrate that Jefferson's belief in the combined power of knowledge, freedom of ideas, and democracy is the Library's true cornerstone.

—*John Y. Cole*
Director
Center for the Book
in the Library of Congress
January 1993

JEFFERSON
THE MAN

T *homas Jefferson was born on April 13, 1743, at Shadwell, Albermarle County, Virginia, and died at Monticello on July 4, 1826, the fiftieth anniversary of the Declaration of Independence. He was a member of the Virginia House of Burgesses, a delegate to the Continental Congress, governor of Virginia, minister to France, secretary of state, and vice president and president of the United States. This work deals with him not as a public figure, but as a man: as a person; a father and grandfather; a friend and neighbor; a gardener; a farmer; a lover of books; a scientist and inventor; and a writer on religion, education, architecture, and freedom.*

In 1769, I became a member of the legislature by the choice of the county in which I lived, and so continued until it was closed by the Revolution. I made one effort in that body for the permission of the emancipation of slaves, which was rejected, and indeed, during the regal government, nothing liberal could expect success. Our minds were circumscribed with narrow limits, by an habitual belief that it was our duty to be subordinate to the mother country in all matters of government, to direct all our labors in subservience to her interests, and even to observe a bigoted intolerance for all religions but hers.

Autobiography   *January 6–July 21, 1821*

On the 1st of January, 1772, I was married to Martha Skelton, widow of Bathurst Skelton and daughter of John Wayles, then 23 years old. Mr. Wayles was a lawyer of much practice, to which he was introduced more by his great industry, punctuality, and practical readiness than to eminence in the science of his profession.

Autobiography   *January 6–July 21, 1821*

If there is a gratification which I envy any people in this world, it is to your country its music. This is the favorite passion of my soul, and fortune has cast my lot in a country where it is in a state of deplorable barbarism.

Letter to Giovanni Fabbroni   *June 8, 1778*

My dear wife died this day at 11:45 A.M.

Account Book   *September 6, 1782*

There is no habit you will value so much as that of walking far without fatigue. I would advise you to take your exercise in the afternoon, not because it is the best time for exercise, for certainly it is not, but because it is the best time to spare from your studies; and habit will soon reconcile it to health and render it nearly as useful as if you gave to that the more precious hours of the day.

Letter to Peter Carr   *August 19, 1785*

I am an enthusiast on the subject of the arts. But it is an enthusiasm of which I am not ashamed, as its object is to improve the taste of my countrymen, to increase their reputation, to reconcile to them the respect of the world, and procure them its praise.

Letter to James Madison   *September 20, 1785*

My Dear Polly: I have not received a letter from you since I came to France. If you knew how much I love you and what pleasure the receipt of your letters gave me at Philadelphia, you would have written to me, or at least have told your aunt what to write, and her goodness would have induced her to take the trouble of writing it. I wish so much to see you that I have desired your uncle and aunt to send you to me. I know, my dear Polly, how sorry you will be, and ought to be, to leave them and your cousins, but your [sister and m]yself cannot live without you, and after a while we will carry you back again to see your friends in Virginia.

Letter to Mary Jefferson   *September 20, 1785*

My history ... would have been as happy a one as I could have asked, could the subject of my affection have been immortal. But all the favors of fortune have been embittered by private losses.

Letter to Elizabeth Blair Thompson   *January 19, 1787*

Your head, my dear friend, is full of notable things; and being better employed, therefore, I do not expect letters from you. I am constantly roving about to see where I have never seen before and shall never see again. In the great cities, I go to see what travelers think alone worthy of being seen, but I make a job of it and generally gulp it all down in a day. On the other hand, I am never satiated with rambling through the fields and farms, examining the culture and cultivators, with a degree of curiosity which makes some to take me for a fool and others to be much wiser than I am.

Letter to Marquis de Lafayette   *April 11, 1787*

All my wishes end, where I hope my days will end, at Monticello. Too many scenes of happiness mingle themselves with all the recollections of my native woods and fields to suffer them to be supplanted in my affection by any other.

Letter to Dr. George Gilmer   *August 12, 1787*

I had rather be shut up in a very modest cottage with my books, my family and a few old friends, dining on simple bacon, and letting the world roll on as it liked, than to occupy the most splendid post, which any human power can give.

Letter to Alexander Donald   *February 7, 1788*

At Dusseldorf I wished for you much. I surely never saw so precious a collection of paintings. Above all things those of Van der Werff affected me the most. His picture of Sarah delivering Agar to Abraham is delicious. I would have agreed to be Abraham though the consequences could have been that I should have been dead five or six thousand years. Carlo Dolce became also a violent favorite. I am so little of a connoisseur that I preferred the works of these authors to the old faded red things of

Reubens. I am but a son of nature, loving what I see and feel, without being able to give a reason, not caring much whether there be one. At Heidelberg I wished for you too. In fact I led you by the hand through the whole garden.

Letter to Maria Cosway　　　　　　　　　　　*April 24, 1788*

I am retired to Monticello, where, in the bosom of my family and surrounded by my books, I enjoy a repose to which I have long been a stranger. My mornings are devoted to correspondence. From breakfast to dinner, I am in my shops, my garden, or on horseback among my farms; from dinner to dark, I give to society and recreation with my neighbors and friends; and from candle light to early bed-time, I read. My health is perfect, and my strength considerably reinforced by the activity of the course I pursue; perhaps it is as great as usually falls to the lot of near sixty-seven years of age. I talk of ploughs and harrows, of seeding and harvesting, with my neighbors, and of politics too, if they choose with as little reserve as the rest of my fellow citizens, and feel, at length, the blessing of being free to say and do as I please, without being responsible for it to any mortal.

Letter to General Tadeusz Kosciusko　　　*February 26, 1810*

I agree with you that there is a natural aristocracy among men. The grounds of this are virtue and talents.

Letter to John Adams　　　　　　　　　　*October 28, 1813*

You ask if I would agree to live my 70 or rather 73 years over again? To which I say yea. I think with you that it is a good world on the whole, and that it has been framed on a principle of benevolence, and more pleasure than pain dealt out to us. There are indeed (who might say nay) gloomy and hypocondriac minds, inhabitants of diseased bodies, disgusted with the present and despairing of the future, always counting that the worst will happen, because it may happen. To these I say how much pain have cost us the evils which have never happened? My temperament is sanguine. I steer my bark with Hope in the head, leaving Fear astern.

Letter to John Adams　　　　　　　　　　　*April 8, 1816*

When all our faculties have left, or are leaving us, one by one, sight, hearing, memory, every avenue of pleasing sensation is closed, and athymy, debility, and mal-aise left in their places; when the friends of our youth are all gone and a generation is risen around us whom we know not, is death an evil?

Letter to John Adams   *June 1, 1822*

This letter will, to you, be one from the dead. The writer will be in the grave before you can weigh its counsels. Your affectionate and excellent father has requested that I would address to you something which might possibly have a favorable influence on the course of life you have to run, and I too, as a namesake, feel an interest in that course. Few words will be necessary, with good dispositions on your part. Adore God. Reverence and cherish your parents. Love your neighbor as yourself, and your country more than yourself. Be just. Be true. Murmur not at the ways of providence. So shall the life into which you have entered be the portal to one of eternal and ineffable bliss. And if to the dead it is permitted to care for the things of this world, every action of your life will be under my regard. Farewell.

Letter to Thomas Jefferson Smith   *February 21, 1825*

A Decalogue of Canons for Observation in Practical Life
1. Never put off till to-morrow what you can do to-day.
2. Never trouble another for what you can do yourself.
3. Never spend your money before you have it.
4. Never buy what you do not want because it is cheap; it will be dear to you.
5. Pride costs us more than hunger, thirst, and cold.
6. We never repent of having eaten too little.
7. Nothing is troublesome that we do willingly.
8. How much pain have cost us the evils which have never happened.
9. Take things always by their smooth handle.
10. When angry, count ten before you speak; if very angry, an hundred.

Letter to Thomas Jefferson Smith   *February 21, 1825*

A Declaration by the Representatives of the UNITED STATES OF AMERICA, in General Congress assembled.

When in the course of human events it becomes necessary for one people to dissolve the political bands which have connected them with another, and to ~~assume among the powers of the earth the~~ separate and equal station to which the laws of nature & of nature's god entitle them, a decent respect to the opinions of mankind requires that they should declare the causes which impel them to the ~~change~~ separation.

We hold these truths to be ~~sacred & undeniable~~ self-evident; that all men are created equal ~~& independent~~, that ~~from that equal creation they derive~~ ~~rights~~ inherent & inalienable, among ~~which~~ these are ~~the preservation of~~ life, & liberty, & the pursuit of happiness; that to secure these ~~ends~~ rights, governments are instituted among men, deriving their just powers from the consent of the governed; that whenever any form of government ~~shall~~ becomes destructive of these ends, it is the right of the people to alter or to abolish it, & to institute new government, laying it's foundation on such principles & organising it's powers in such form, as to them shall seem most likely to effect their safety & happiness. prudence indeed will dictate that governments long established should not be changed for light & transient causes: and accordingly all experience hath shewn that mankind are more disposed to suffer while evils are sufferable, than to right themselves by abolishing the forms to which they are accustomed. but when a long train of abuses & usurpations [begun at a distinguished period, &] pursuing invariably the same object, evinces a design to ~~subject reduce~~ them ~~under absolute Despotism~~, it is their right, it is their duty, to throw off such ~~government~~ + & to provide new guards for their future security. such has been the patient sufferance of these colonies; & such is now the necessity which constrains them to expunge their former systems of government. the history of the present king of great Britain is a history of ~~unremitting~~ injuries and usurpations [among which appears no solitary fact to contra- dict the uniform tenor of the rest all of which have] in direct object the establishment of an absolute tyranny over these states. to prove this, let facts be submitted to a candid world [for the truth of which we pledge a faith yet unsullied by falsehood]

JEFFERSON
ON AMERICA

A *lthough Thomas Jefferson was a friend of all man-*
kind and a citizen of the world, his special love of
America is shown in the following selections. He believed in
progress, that things would get better in economic, religious,
and personal freedom. Perhaps no other American has had
such a lasting influence on this country.

We are not to expect to be translated from despotism to liberty in a featherbed.

Letter to Marquis de Lafayette   *April 2, 1790*

This morning at Mt. Vernon I had the following conversation with the President. ... I told him that as far as I knew there was but one voice there which was for his continuance. That as to myself I had ever preferred the pursuits of private life to those of public, which had nothing in them agreeable to me. I explained to him the circumstances of the war which had first called me from a retirement on which I had determined. That I had constantly kept my eye on my own home and could no longer refrain from returning to it; as to himself his presence was important, that he was the only man in the U.S. who possessed the confidence of the whole; that government was founded in opinion and confidence; and that the longer he remained, the stronger would become the habits of the people in submitting to the government and in thinking it a thing to be maintained.

Notes on a Conversation with George Washington   *October 1, 1792*

Our geographical distance is insensible still to foreigners. They consider America the size of a [garden] of which Massachusetts is one square and Virginia another.

Letter to John Adams   *May 27, 1795*

The first object of my heart is my own country. In that is embarked my family, my fortune, and my own existence. I have not one farthing of interest, nor one fibre of attachment out of it, nor a single motive of preference of any one nation to another, but in proportion as they are more or less friendly to us.

Letter to Elbridge Gerry   *January 26, 1799*

A rising nation, spread over a wise and fruitful land, traversing all the seas with the rich productions of their industry, engaged in commerce with nations who feel power and forget right, advancing rapidly to destinies beyond the reach of mortal eye.

First Inauguration Address   *March 4, 1801*

Agriculture, manufactures, commerce, and navigation, the four pillars of our prosperity, are the most thriving when left most free to Individual enterprise.

First Annual Message to Congress   *December 8, 1801*

When we consider that this government is charged with the external and mutual relations only of these states; that the states themselves have principal care of our persons, our property, and our reputation, constituting the great field of human concerns, we may well doubt whether our organization is not too complicated, too expensive; whether offices and officers have not been multiplied unnecessarily and sometimes injuriously to the service they were meant to promote.

First Annual Message to Congress   *December 8, 1801*

Brothers of the Choctaw Nation: We have long heard of your nation as a numerous, peaceable, and friendly people, but this is the first visit we have had from its great men at the seat of government. I welcome you here and am glad to take you by the hand and to assure you, for your nation, that we are their friends. Born in the same land, we ought to live as brothers, doing to each other all the good we can and not listening to wicked men, who may endeavor to make us enemies. By living in peace, we can help and prosper one another; by waging war, we can kill and destroy many on both sides; but those who survive will not be happier for that. Then, brothers, let it forever be peace and good

neighborhood between us.
Address to the Brothers of the Choctaw Nation December 17, 1803

Taking all these together, I prefer much the climate of the United States to that of Europe. I think it a more cheerful one. It is our cloudless sky which has eradicated from our constitutions all disposition to hang ourselves, which we might otherwise have inherited from our English ancestors.
Letter to Constantine François de Volney *February 8, 1805*

I carry with me the consolation of a firm persuasion that Heaven has in store for our beloved country long ages to come of prosperity and happiness.
Eighth (and Final) Annual Message to Congress *November 8, 1808*

A strict observance of the written laws is doubtless one of the high duties of a good citizen, but it is not the highest. The laws of necessity, of self-preservation, of saving our country when in danger, are of higher obligation. To lose our country by a scrupulous adherence to written law would be to lose the law itself, with life, liberty, property, and all those who are enjoying them with us, thus absurdly sacrificing the end to the means.
Letter to John B. Colvin *September 20, 1810*

It is a wise rule and should be fundamental in a government disposed to cherish its credit, and at the same time to restrain the use of it within the limits of its faculties, "never to borrow a dollar without laying a tax in the same instant for paying the interest annually, and the principal within a given term; and to consider that tax as pledged to the creditors on public faith." On such a pledge as this, sacredly observed, a government may always command, on a reasonable interest, all the lendable money of their citizens, while the necessity of an equivalent tax is a salutary warning to them and their constituents against oppressions, bankruptcy, and its inevitable consequence, revolution. But the terms of redemption must be moderate, and at any rate within the limits of their rightful powers. But what limits, it will be asked, does this prescribe to their powers? What is to hinder them from creating a perpetual debt? The laws of nature, I answer. The earth belongs to the living, not to the dead.

Letter to John Wayles Eppes   *June 24, 1813*

My opinion has ever been that, until more can be done for them, we should endeavor, with those whom fortune has thrown on our hands, to feed and clothe them well, protect them from ill usage, require such reasonable labor only as it is performed voluntarily by freemen, and be led by no repugnancies to abdicate them and our duties to them.

Letter to Edward Coles   *August 25, 1814*

I ... place economy among the first and most important republican virtues, and public debt as the greatest of the dangers to be feared.

Letter to William Plumer   *July 21, 1816*

The kind invitation I receive from you, on the part of the citizens of the city of Washington, to be present with them at their celebration on the fiftieth anniversary of American Independence, as one of the surviving signers of an instrument pregnant with our own, and the fate of the world, is most flattering to myself and heightened by the honorable accompaniment proposed for the comfort of such a journey. ... May it be to the world, what I believe it will be (to some parts sooner, to others later, but finally to all), the signal of arousing men to burst the chains under which monkish ignorance and superstition had persuaded them to bind themselves and to assume the blessings and security of self-government. That form which we have substituted restores the free right to the unbounded exercise of reason and freedom of opinion. All eyes are opened, or opening, to the rights of man. The general spread of the light of science has already laid open to every view the palpable truth, that the mass of mankind has not been born with saddles on their backs, nor a favored few booted and spurred, ready to ride them legitimately by the grace of God. These are grounds of hope for others. For ourselves, let the annual return of this day forever refresh our recollections of these rights and an undiminished devotion to them.

Last Letter to Roger Weightman   *June 24, 1826*

JEFFERSON
ON EXPLORATION

J efferson visited much of the country, including Vir-
ginia, Pennsylvania, New York, and New England.
He was interested in the West long before the Louisiana
Purchase on both political and scientific grounds. While
Louisiana was still French, Jefferson obtained $2,500 from
Congress for an expedition to explore the source of the
Missouri River and the regions west to the Pacific coast. His
secretary, Meriwether Lewis, was chosen to lead the expedi-
tion with William Clark as second in command. The
expedition left St. Louis on May 14, 1804, and returned on
September 23, 1806. He sent Zebulon Pike to find the source
of the Mississippi, and subsequently west to the Rockies.
Jefferson's vision of the West influenced explorers for the next
half century.

Surely never did [a] small hero experience greater misad-
ventures than I did on the first two or three days of my traveling.
Twice did my horse run away with me and greatly endanger the
breaking of my neck on the first day. On the second I drove two
hours through as copious a rain as I have ever seen without
meeting with a single house to which I could repair for shelter.
On the third, in going through Pamunkey, being unacquainted
with the ford, I passed through water so deep as to run over the
cushion as I sat on it, and to add to the danger, at that Instant one
wheel mounted a rock which I was confident was as high as the
axle and rendered it necessary for me to exercise all my skill in
the doctrine of gravity.

Letter to John Page   *May 25, 1766*

I find they have subscribed a very large sum of money in
England for exploring the country from the Mississippi to

California. They pretend it is only to promote knowledge. I am afraid they have thoughts of colonising into that quarter. Some of us have been talking here in a feeble way of making the attempt to search the country. But I doubt whether we have enough of that kind of spirit to raise the money. How would you like to lead such a party?

Letter to George Rogers Clark   *December 4, 1783*

My last accounts of Ledyard were from Grand Cairo. He was just ... plunging into the unknown regions of Africa, probably never to emerge again. If he returns, he has promised me to go to America and penetrate from Kentucky to the western side of the continent.

Letter to William Carmichael   *March 4, 1789*

We were more pleased, however, with the botanical objects which continually presented themselves [in New York]. Those either unknown or rare in Virginia were the sugar maple in vast abundance; the silver fir; white pine; pitch pine; spruce pine; a shrub with decumbent stems, which they call Juniper; an azalea, very different from nudiflora, with very large clusters of flowers more thickly set on the branches, of a deeper red and high pink-fragrance, it is the richest shrub I have ever seen; the honey-suckle of the gardens growing wild on the banks of Lake George; the paper-birch, an aspen with a velvet leaf; a shrub-willow with downy catkins; a wild goose berry; the wild cherry with single fruit (not the bunch cherry); strawberries in abundance.

Letter to Thomas Mann Randolph   *June 5, 1791*

The object of your mission is to explore the Missouri River and such principal stream of it, as by its source and communication with the waters of the Pacific Ocean, whether the Columbia, Oregon, Colorado, or any other river, may offer the most direct and practicable water communication across this continent for the purposes of commerce.

Beginning at the mouth of the Missouri, you will take observations of latitude and longitude at all remarkable points on the river, and especially at the mouths of rivers, at rapids, at islands, and other places and objects distinguished by such natural marks and characters of a durable kind, as that they may with certainty be recognized hereafter. The courses of the river between these points of observation may be supplied by the compass, the logline, and by the time, corrected by the observations themselves. The variations of the compass, too, in different places should be noticed.

Instructions to Captain Meriwether Lewis   *June 20, 1803*

You will therefore endeavor to make yourself acquainted, as far as a diligent pursuit of your journey shall admit, with the names of the nations and their numbers; the extent and limits of their possessions; their relations with other tribes or nations; their language, traditions, monuments; their ordinary occupations in agriculture, fishing, hunting, war, arts, and the implements for these; their food, clothing, and domestic accommodations; the diseases prevalent among them and the remedies they use; moral and physical circumstance which distinguish them from the tribes they know.

Instructions to Captain Meriwether Lewis   *June 20, 1803*

Other objects worthy of notice will be the soil and face of the country, its growth and vegetable productions, especially those not of the United States; the animals of the country generally, and especially those not known in the United States; the remains and accounts of any which may be deemed rare or extinct; the mineral productions of every kind, but more particularly metals, limestone, pit coal, and saltpeter; salines and mineral waters, noting the temperature of the last and such circumstances as may indicate their character; volcanic appearances; climate as characterized by the thermometer, by the proportion of rainy, cloudy, and clear days, by lightning, hail, snow, ice, by the access and recess of frost, by the winds, prevailing at different seasons; the dates at which particular plants put forth or lose their flowers, or leaf; times of appearance of particular birds, reptiles, or insects.

Instructions to Captain Meriwether Lewis   *June 20, 1803*

In all your intercourse with the natives, treat them in the most friendly and conciliatory manner which their own conduct will admit; allay all jealousies as to the object of your journey, satisfy them of its own innocence; make them acquainted with the position, extent, character, peaceable and commercial dispositions of the United States; of our wish to be neighborly, friendly, and useful to them; and of our dispositions to a commercial intercourse with them; confer with them on the points most convenient, as mutual emporiums and the articles of most desirable interchange for them and us. If a few of their influential chiefs, within practicable distance, wish to visit us, arrange such a visit with them, and furnish them with authority to call on our officers, on their entering the United States, to have them conveyed to this place at public expense. If any of them should wish to have some of their young people brought up with us and taught such arts as may be useful to them, we will receive, instruct, and take care of them.

Instructions to Captain Meriwether Lewis   *June 20, 1803*

Our last news of Captain Lewis was that he had reached the upper of the Missouri, and had taken horses to cross the highlands to the Columbia River. ... These expeditions are so laborious and hazardous that men of science, used to the temperature and inactivity of their closet, cannot be induced to undertake them. They are headed therefore by persons qualified expressly to give us the geography of the rivers with perfect accuracy, and of good common knowledge and observation in the animal, vegetable, and mineral departments.

Letter to Constantine François de Volney   *February 11, 1806*

The expedition of Messrs. Lewis and Clarke, for exploring the river Missouri, and the best communication from that to the Pacific Ocean, had all the success which could have been expected. They have traced the Missouri nearly to its source, descended the Columbia to the Pacific Ocean, ascertained with accuracy the geography of that interesting communication across our continent, learned the character of the country, of its commerce, and inhabitants; and it is but justice to say that Messrs. Lewis and Clarke, and their brave companions, have by this arduous service deserved well of their country.

Sixth Annual Message to Congress   *December 2, 1806*

JEFFERSON
ON DEMOCRACY

J efferson's beliefs can be found in the Declaration of Independence: "That all men are created equal; that they are endowed by their creator with certain unalienable rights; that among these are Life, Liberty, and the Pursuit of Happiness" and in his first inaugural address, presented on March 4, 1801, which ranks among the best and most important of the presidential addresses. In it he made a plea for conciliation and spoke of unity, tolerance, hope in the future, and a philosophy of government.

I am persuaded myself that the good sense of the people will always be found to be the best army. They may be led astray for a moment, but will soon correct themselves. ... The basis of our government being the opinion of the people, the first object should be to keep that right; and were it left to me to decide whether we should have a government without newspapers or newspapers without a government, I should not hesitate a moment to prefer the latter. But I should mean that every man should receive those papers and be capable of reading them.

Letter to Colonel Edward Carrington   *January 16, 1787*

Whenever the people are well informed, they can be trusted with their own government; that whenever things get so far wrong as to attract their notice, they may be relied on to set them to rights.

Letter to Dr. Richard Price   *January 8, 1789*

In every free and deliberating society, there must, from the nature of man, be opposite parties and violent dissensions and discords; and one of these, for the most part, must prevail over the other for a longer or shorter time. Perhaps this party division is necessary to induce each to watch and delate to the people the proceedings of the other.

Letter to John Taylor   *June 1, 1798*

Still one thing more, fellow citizens—a wise and frugal government, which shall restrain men from injuring one another, which shall leave them otherwise free to regulate their own pursuits of industry and improvement, and shall not take from the mouth of labor the bread it has earned. This is the sum of good government, and this is necessary to close the circle of our felicities.

First Inaugural Address   *March 4, 1801*

All, too, will bear in mind this sacred principle, that though the will of the majority is in all cases to prevail, that will, to be rightful, must be reasonable; that the minority possess their equal rights, which equal laws must protect, and to violate which would be oppression.

First Inaugural Address   *March 4, 1801*

Sometimes it is said that man cannot be trusted with the government of himself. Can he, then, be trusted with the government of others? Or have we found angels in the forms of kings to govern him? Let history answer the question.

First Inaugural Address   *March 4, 1801*

Freedom of religion, freedom of the press, and freedom of person under the protection of the habeas corpus, and trial by juries impartially selected. These principles form the bright constellation which has gone before us and guided our steps through an age of revolution and reformation. The wisdom of our sages and the blood of our heroes have been devoted to their attainment. They should be the creed of our political faith, the text of civil instruction, the touchstone by which we try the services of those we trust; and should we wander from them in moments of error or alarm, let us hasten to retrace our steps and to regain the road which leads to peace, liberty, and safety.

First Inaugural Address   *March 4, 1801*

The care of human life and happiness, and not their destruction, is the first and only legitimate object of good government.

Letter to the Republican Citizens   *August 4, 1811*
of Washington County, Maryland

The idea of representative government has taken root and growth among them. Their masters feel it and are saving themselves by timely offers of this modification of their own powers. Belgium, Prussia, Poland, Lombardy, etc. are now offered a representative organization, illusive probably at first, but it will grow into power in the end. Opinion is power, and that opinion will come.

Letter to John Adams   *January 11, 1816*

No man has a natural right to commit aggression on the equal rights of another, and this is all from which the laws ought to restrain him; every man is under the natural duty of contributing to the necessities of society, and this is all the laws should enforce on him; and no man having a natural right to be the judge between himself and another, it is his natural duty to submit to the umpirage of an impartial third.

Letter to Francis Walker Gilmer   *June 7, 1816*

Some men look at constitutions with sanctimonious reverance and deem them like the ark of the covenant, too sacred to be touched. They ascribe to the men of the preceding age a wisdom more than human and suppose what they did to be beyond amendment. I knew that age well; I belonged to it and labored with it. It deserved well of its country. It was very like the present, but without the experience of the present; and forty years of experience in government is worth a century of book-reading; and this they would say themselves, were they to rise from the dead.

I am certainly not an advocate for frequent and untried changes in laws and constitutions. I think moderate imperfections had better be borne with because, when once known, we accommodate ourselves to them and find practical means of correcting their ill effects. But I know also that laws and institutions must go hand in hand with the progress of the human mind. As that becomes more developed, more enlightened, as new discoveries are made, new truths disclosed, and manners and opinions change with the change of circumstances, institutions must advance also and keep pace with the times.

Letter to Samuel Kercheval   *July 12, 1816*

I know of no safe depository of the ultimate powers of the society but the people themselves; and if we think them not enlightened enough to exercise their control with a wholesome discretion, the remedy is not [to] take it from them, but to inform their discretion.

Letter to William Charles Jarvis   *September 28, 1820*

And even should the cloud of barbarism and despotism again obscure the science and liberties of Europe, this country remains to preserve and restore light and liberty to them. In short, the flames kindled on the Fourth of July 1776. have spread over too much of the globe to be extinguished by the feeble engines of despotism. On the contrary they will consume those engines and all who work them.

Letter to John Adams   *September 12, 1821*

Men by their constitution are naturally divided into two parties: 1.) Those who fear and distrust the people, and wish to draw all powers from them into the hands of the higher classes. 2.) Those who identify themselves with the people, have confidence in them, cherish and consider them as the most honest and safe, although not the most wise depository of the public interests. In every country these two parties exist; and in every one where they are free to think, speak, and write, they will declare themselves.

Letter to Henry Lee   *August 10, 1824*

A good cause is often injured more by ill-timed efforts of its friends than by the arguments of its enemies. Persuasion, perseverance, and patience are the best advocates of questions depending on the wills of others.

Letter to James Heaton   *May 20, 1826*

JEFFERSON
ON GARDENING

*T*homas Jefferson loved gardening and for over fifty-
eight years kept a garden journal. In 1766, he started
his garden journal with the following entry: "March 30,
Purple hyacinth begins to bloom." His last entry was in
1824, noting the planting and harvest dates of spinach,
cucumbers, and squashes. He experimented with a green-
house and had numerous flower beds. His 1,000-foot-long
garden at Monticello is a beautiful sampler of nineteenth-
century plants.

The laboring people here are poorer than in England.
They pay about one half their produce in rent; the English, in
general, about a third. The gardening in that country is the
article in which it surpasses all the earth. I mean their pleasure
gardening.

Letter to John Page   *May 4, 1786*

Having decisively made up my mind for retirement at the
end of my present term, my views and attentions are all turned
homewards. I have hitherto been engaged in my buildings,
which will be furnished in the course of the present year. The
improvement of my grounds has been reserved for my occupation on my return home. For this reason it is that I have put off
to the fall of the year after next the collection of such curious
trees as will bear our winters in the open air.

The grounds which I destine to improve in the style of the
English gardens are in a form very difficult to be managed. They
comprise the northern quadrant of a mountain for about two-
thirds of its height and then spread for the upper third over its
whole crown. They contain about three hundred acres, washed
at the foot for about a mile by a river of the size of the Schuylkill.

The hill is generally too steep for direct ascent, but we make level walks successively along its side, which in its upper part encircle the hill and intersect these again by others of easy ascent in various parts. They are chiefly still in their native woods, which are majestic and are very generally a close undergrowth, which I have not suffered to be touched, knowing how much easier it is to cut away than to fill up.

Letter to William Hamilton   *July 1806*

My Dear Anne: I wrote yesterday to your Mama and mentioned what I should send to your charge by Davy, for fear I might be prevented from writing to you by him. I have just time to say that I have sent the following articles.

1. A small pot containing several sprigs of Geranium, stuck round as a plant supposed to be Orange.
2. A long earthen box of Monthly strawberries, which I pray you to take care of till spring when we will plant them at Monticello. The gardener says they need never be watered during winter. Yet I should think a little stale water in warm weather from time to time would be safest.
3. A bag of paccan nuts (about 100.) for your papa for planting. I am this moment called off, therefore Adieu my dear Anne.

Letter to Anne Cary Randolph   *November 24, 1807*

I promised to stock you with the Alpine strawberry as soon as my beds would permit. I now send you a basket of plants and can spare you ten baskets more if you desire it. Their value, you know, is the giving strawberries eight months in the year. But they require a large piece of ground and therefore I am moving them into the truck patch, as I cannot afford them room enough in the garden. I have received from McMahon some plants of the true Hudson strawberry. The last rains have brought them forward and ensured their living. I have been twenty years trying unsuccessfully to get them here. The next year I shall be able to stock you. I have received also from McMahon four plants of his wonderful gooseberry. I measured the fruit of them 3. I[nches] round. By the next year I hope they will afford you cuttings.

Letter to George Divers   *March 10, 1812*

I closed the year before last a seven years' course of observations intended to characterize the climate of this State, which though very various in its various parts may be considered as reduced to a mean at this place nearly central to the whole. In return for your favor I transcribe the heads of observation which I thought requisite and some of the general result with the assurance of my high respect and esteem.

1. The greatest and least height of the thermometer every day.
2. The number of freezing nights in winter (50) and of freezing days (10).
3. The earliest frost in autumn Oct. 7–26, and the latest in spring Mar.19–May 1.
4. The earliest ice in autumn Oct. 24–Nov. 15, and latest in spring Mar. 8–Apr. 10.
5. The quantity of water falling in a year, average 47.218.
6. The number of rains in the year, 89.
7. The number of fair days average 5 to the week.
8. The number of snow 22 1/2 inches average covers the ground 22 days.
9. The flowering of plants, ripening of their fruit and coming to the table of the products of the garden, arrival of birds, insects, etc.

> The peach blossoms Mar. 9–Apr. 4.
> The house martin Mar. 18–Apr. 9.
> Asparagus come to table Mar. 23–Apr. 14.
> The lilac blooms Apr. 1–Apr. 28.
> The red bud blooms Apr. 2–19.
> The whip-poor-will is heard Apr. 2–21.
> The dogwood blossoms Apr. 3–22.
> The locust blossoms Apr. 25–May 17.
> Garden pea comes to table (unforced) May 3–25.
> Strawberries ripe May 3–25.
> Fireflies appear May 8.
> Cherries ripe May 18–25.
> Wheat harvest begins June 21–29.
> Cucumbers at table (unforced) June 22–25.
> Peaches ripe July 7–21.
> Katydids or sawyers heard July 14–20.

Letter to Jacob Bigelow   *April 11, 1818*

Thomas Jefferson

The soil in this part of the country is as fertile as any upland soil in any of the maritime States, inhabited fully by substantial yeomanry of farmers (tobacco long since given up), and being at the first ridge of mountains there is not a healthier or more genial climate in the world. Our maximum of heat and that only one or two days in summer is about 96°, the minimum in winter is 5 1/2°, but the mean of the months of June, July, August is 72°, 75°, 73°, and of December, January, February is 45°, 36°, 40°. The thermometer is below 55° (the fire point) four months of the year and about a month before and after that we require fire in the mornings and evenings. Our average of snow is 22 inches, covering the ground as many days in the winter.

Letter to Nathaniel Bowditch   *October 26, 1818*

My Dear Ellen: Your letter of the 8th. was received the day before yesterday, and as the season for engrafting is passing rapidly by, I will not detain the apple cuttings for Mr. Gray (but until I may have other matter for writing a big letter to you) I send a dozen cuttings, as much as a letter can protect, by our 1st. mail, and wish they may retain their vitality until they reach him. They are called the Taliaferro apple, being from a seedling tree, discovered by a gentleman of that name near Williamsburg, and yield unquestionably the finest cyder we have ever known, and more like wine than any liquor I have ever tasted which was not wine. If it is worth reminding me of the ensuing winter, I may send a larger supply, and in better times through Colonel Peyton.

Letter to Ellen Randolph Coolidge *March 19, 1826*

You perhaps noticed in the newspapers some three or four months ago the mention of cucumbers in a particular garden in Ohio which measured 2 1/2 f[eet] and 3 f[eet] length. Having a friend in that quarter, I wrote and requested him to procure and send me some seed from one of the identical cucumbers. He has sent it, and to multiply chances of securing it, I send you 9. seeds, assured that nobody will be more likely to succeed than yourself.

Letter to George Divers   *April 22, 1826*

JEFFERSON ON FARMING

*T homas Jefferson was a farmer who lived on the income
from his farms. His crops included wheat, rye, oats,
barley, and corn; grasses and hay for fodder; and flax and
hemp for spinning and weaving. He raised horses, cattle,
mules, oxen, sheep, and hogs. He had an extensive orchard
of four hundred trees. He described his agricultural theories
and experiences to George Washington, John Adams, James
Madison, Henry Knox, Lafayette, and a variety of other
correspondents, and kept a farm book from 1774 until a few
weeks before his death in 1826.*

In Europe the lands are either cultivated or locked up
against the cultivator. Manufacture must therefore be resorted
of necessity not of choice, and support the surplus of their
people. But we have an immensity of land courting the industry
of the husbandman. Is it best then that all our citizens should be
employed in its improvement, or that one half should be called
off from that to exercise manufacture and handicraft arts for the
other? Those who labour in the earth are the chosen people of
God, if ever he had a chosen people, whose breasts he has made
his peculiar deposit for substantial and genuine virtue. It is the
focus in which he keeps alive that sacred fire, which otherwise
might escape from the face of the earth.

Notes on the State of Virginia   *1781–1785*

The indifferent state of agriculture among us does not
proceed from a want of knowledge merely; it is from our having
such quantities of land to waste as we please. In Europe the
object is to make the most of their land, labor being abundant;
here it is to make the most of our labor, land being abundant.

Notes on the State of Virginia   *1781–1785*

When at Mount Vernon, on my way here, I asked of the President what his rotation of crops were. He told me it was of seven years, to wit: 1. Corn and potatoes. 2. Wheat. 3. Buckwheat to be plowed in. 4. Wheat. 5.6.7. clover. His corn and potatoes are in hills alternatively 4 f[eet] apart, and the alternation being in the cross row as well as the other, distances his corn to near 6 feet. He says he makes as much corn as if there were no potatoes, and much more potatoes than corn. He is of the opinion that a crop of potatoes improves the ground. His mixture of corn and potatoes would perhaps be a good way of introducing potatoes into use in the farm.

Letter to Thomas Mann Randolph, Jr.   *October 19, 1792*

I return to farming with an ardour which I scarcely knew in my youth, and which has got the better entirely of my love of study. Instead of writing ten or twelve letters a day, which I have been in the habit of doing as a thing of course, I put off answering my letters now, farmer-like, till a rainy day, and then find it sometimes postponed by other necessary occupations.

Letter to John Adams   *April 25, 1794*

If you visit me as a farmer, it must be as a co-disciple, for I am but a learner, an eager one indeed but yet desperate, being too old now to learn a new art. However, I am as much delighted and occupied with it as if I was the greatest adept. I shall talk with you about it from morning till night, and put you on very short allowance as to political aliment. Now and then a pious ejaculation for the French and Dutch republicans, returning with due dispatch to clover, potatoes, wheat, etc.

Letter to William Branch Giles   *April 27, 1795*

Have you become a farmer? Is it not pleasanter than to be shut up within four walls and delving eternally with the pen? I am become the most ardent farmer in the state. I live on my horse from morning to night almost. Intervals are filled up with attentions to a nailery I carry on. I rarely look into a book, and more rarely take up a pen. I have proscribed newspapers, not taking a single one, nor scarcely ever looking into one. My next reformation will be to allow neither pen, ink, nor paper to be kept on the farm. When I have accomplished this, I shall be in a fair way of indemnifying myself for the drudgery in which I have passed my life. If you are half as much delighted with the farm as I am, you bless your stars at your riddance from public cares.

Letter to General Henry Knox   *June 1, 1795*

I put away this disgusting dish of old fragments and talk to you of my peas and clover. As to the latter article, I have great encouragement from the friendly nature of our soil. I think I have had, both the last and present year, as good clover from common grounds, which had brought several crops of wheat and corn without ever having been manured, as I ever saw on the lots around Philadelphia. I verily believe that a yield of thirty-four acres, sowed on wheat April was twelve-month, has given me a ton to the acre at its first cutting this spring. The stalks extended measured 3 1/2 feet long very commonly. Another field, a year older, and which yielded as well the last year, has sensibly fallen off this year. My exhausted fields bring a clover not high enough for hay, but I hope to make seed from it. ... Our wheat and rye are generally fine, and the prices talked of bid fair to indemnify us for the poor crops of the last two years.

Letter to George Washington   *June 19, 1796*

The class principally defective is that of agriculture. It is the first in utility and ought to be the first in respect. The same artificial means which have been used to produce a competition in learning may be equally successful restoring agriculture to its primary dignity in the eyes of men. It is a science of the very first order. It counts among its handmaids the most respected sciences, such as Chemistry, Natural Philosophy, Mechanics, Mathematics generally, Natural History, Botany. In every College and University, a professor of agriculture, and the class of its students, might be honored as the first.

Letter to David Williams   *November 14, 1803*

We could, in the United States, make as great a variety of wines as are made in Europe, not exactly of the same kinds, but doubtless as good.

Letter to C. P. de Lasteyrie   *July 15, 1808*

I have often thought that if heaven had given me choice of my position and calling, it should have been on a rich spot on earth, well watered and near a good market for the production of the garden. No occupation is so delightful to me as the culture of the earth, and no culture comparable to that of the garden. Such a variety of subjects, some always coming to perfection, the failure of one thing repaired by the success of another, and instead of one harvest a continued one through the year. Under a total want of demand except for our family table, I am still devoted to the garden. But though an old man, I am but a young gardener.

Letter to Charles Willson Peale   *August 20, 1811*

The spontaneous energies of the earth are a gift of nature, but they require the labor of man to direct their operation. And the question is so to husband his labor as to turn the greatest quantity of the earth to his benefit. Ploughing deep, your recipe for killing weeds is also the recipe for almost every good thing in farming. The plow is to the farmer what the wand is to the sorcerer. Its effect is really like sorcery. In the country wherein I live, we have discovered a new use for it, equal in value to its services before known. Our country is hilly and we have been in the habit of ploughing in strait rows whether up or down hill, in oblique lines, or however they lead, and our soil was all rapidly running into the rivers. We now plough horizontally following the curvatures of the hills and hollows on the dead level, however crooked the lines may be. Every furrow thus acts as a reservoir to receive and retain the waters, all of which go to the benefit of the growing plant instead of running off into streams.

Letter to Charles Willson Peale   *March 17, 1813*

Our agriculture presents little interesting. Wheat looks badly, much having been killed by the late severe weather. Corn is scarce, but its price kept down to 3. D. by the substitute of wheat as food both for laborers and horses, costing only 3/6 to 4/. They begin to distill the old flour, getting ten galls. of whiskey from the barrel and consequently more than we can get at Richmond for the new.

Letter to James Madison   *March 10, 1814*

JEFFERSON
ON INDEPENDENCE

J efferson was a member of the Virginia House of Burgesses from 1769–1776, promoting various measures to resist British authority. In 1774, he wrote the instructions—later published as A Summary View of the Rights of British America—*to the Virginia delegates to the First Continental Congress. In 1776, he wrote a draft constitution for Virginia, proposing an independent government. At the Second Continental Congress in Philadelphia, Richard Henry Lee of Virginia moved a resolution for independence. On June 7, 1776, a committee was appointed by the Congress to draft a statement on the reasons for separation from England. The committee included John Adams, Benjamin Franklin, Thomas Jefferson, Robert Livingston, and Roger Sherman, but it was Jefferson who prepared a first draft and submitted it to the others for review. Changes were made after it was presented to the Congress on June 28, but the words remain largely those of Jefferson. He continued to work for freedom throughout his life.*

The inhabitants of the several States of British America are subject to the laws which they adopted at their first settlement, and to such others as have since been made by their respective Legislatures, duly constituted and appointed with their own consent. No other Legislature whatever can rightly exercise authority over them; and these privileges they hold as the common rights of mankind, confirmed by the political constitutions they have respectively assumed and also by several charters of compact from the Crown.

Resolution of Albemarle County   *July 26, 1774*

We hold these truths to be self-evident: that all men are created equal; that they are endowed by their Creator with certain unalienable Rights; that among these are Life, Liberty, and the pursuit of Happiness; that to secure these rights, Governments are instituted among Men, deriving their just powers from the consent of the governed; that whenever any Form of Government becomes destructive of these ends, it is the Right of the People to alter or to abolish it, and to institute new Government, laying its foundation on such principles, and organizing its powers in such form, as to seem most likely to effect their Safety and Happiness. Prudence, indeed, will dictate that Governments long established should not be changed for light and transient causes; and accordingly all experience hath shown that mankind are more disposed to suffer, while evils are sufferable, than to right themselves by abolishing the forms to which they are accustomed. But when a long train of abuses and usurpations, pursuing invariably the same Object, evinces a design to reduce them under absolute Despotism, it is their right, it is their duty, to throw off such Government, and to provide new Guards for their future security.

Declaration of Independence *July 4, 1776*

We, therefore, the Representatives of the United States of America, in General Congress, Assembled, appealing to the Supreme Judge of the world for the rectitude of our intentions, do, in the Name, and by Authority of the good People of these colonies, solemnly publish and declare that these United Colonies are, and of Right ought to be Free and Independent States; that they are absolved from all Allegiance to the British Crown; and that all political connection between them and the State of Great Britain is and ought to be totally dissolved; and that as Free and Independent States, they have full Power to levy War, conclude Peace, contract Alliances, establish Commerce, and to do all other Acts and Things which Independent States may of right do. And for the support of this Declaration with a firm reliance on the Protection of Divine Providence, we mutually pledge to each other our Lives, our Fortunes, and our sacred Honor.

Declaration of Independence *July 4, 1776*

Experience hath shown that even under the best forms [of government], those entrusted with power have, in time, and by slow operations, perverted it into tyranny; and it is believed that the most effectual means of preventing this would be to illuminate, as far as practicable, the minds of the people at large, and more especially to give them knowledge of those facts, which history exhibiteth, that possessed thereby of the experience of other ages and countries, they may be enabled to know ambition under all its shapes and prompt them to exhibit their natural powers to defeat its purposes.

A Bill for the More General Diffusion of Knowledge   June 18, 1779

The whole commerce between master and slave is a perpetual exercise of the most boisterous passions, the most unremitting despotism on the one part and degrading submissions on the other. Our children see this and learn to imitate it, for man is an imitative animal. This quality is the germ of all education in him. … And with what execration should the statesman be loaded, who permitting one half the citizens thus to trample on the rights of the other, transforms those into despots and these into enemies.

Notes on the State of Virginia   *1781–1785*

I hold it that a little rebellion, now and then, is a good thing, and as necessary in the political world as storms in the physical.

Letter to James Madison   *January 30, 1787*

The ground of liberty is to be gained by inches. We must be contented to secure what we can get from time to time and eternally press forward for what is yet to get. It takes time to persuade men to do what is for their own good.

Letter to Rev. Charles Clay   *January 27, 1790*

I received with great pleasure the present of your pamphlets, as well for the thing itself as that it was a testimony of your recollection. Would you believe it possible that in this country there should be high and important characters who need your lessons in republicanism and who do not heed them? It is but too true that we have a sect preaching up and pouting after an English constitution of kings, lords, and commons, and whose heads are itching for crowns, coronets, and mitres. But our people, my good friend, are firm and unanimous in their principles of republicanism and there is no better proof of it than they love what you write and read it with delight. ... Go on then in doing with your pen what in other times was done with the sword; shew that reformation is more practicable by operating on the mind than on the body of man.

> *Letter to Thomas Paine*   *June 19, 1792*

I have sworn upon the altar of God eternal hostility against every form of tyranny over the minds of man.

> *Letter to Dr. Benjamin Rush*   *September 23, 1800*

I receive with great satisfaction the visit you have been so kind as to make us at this place, and I thank the Great Spirit who has conducted you to us in health and safety. It is well that friends should sometimes meet, open their minds mutually, and renew the chain of affection. Made by the same Great Spirit and living in the same land with our brothers, the red men, we consider ourselves as of the same family; we wish to live with them as one people and to cherish their interests as our own. The evils which of necessity encompass the life of man are sufficiently numerous. Why should we add to them by voluntarily distressing and destroying one another? Peace, brothers, is better than war.

> *Address to Brothers and Friends of the Miamis,*   *January 7, 1802*
> *Powtewatamies, and Weeauks*

If a nation expects to be ignorant and free, in a state of civilization, it expects what never was and never will be.

> *Letter to Colonel Charles Yancey*   *January 6, 1816*

Nothing is more certainly written in the book of fate than that these people are to be free; nor is it less certain that the two races, equally free, cannot live in the same government. Nature, habit, opinion have drawn indelible lines of distinction between them. It is still in our power to direct the process of emancipation and deportation peaceably, and in such slow degree, as that the evil will wear off insensibly and their place be, *pari passu*, filled up by free white laborers. If, on the contrary, it is left to force itself on, human nature must shudder at the prospect held up.

> *Autobiography*   *January 6–July 21, 1821*

JEFFERSON ON
SCIENCE AND TECHNOLOGY

T homas Jefferson was a keen observer of the natural
world. As a student at the College of William and
Mary, he developed an interest in physics and mathematics;
this interest expanded to include celestial mechanics, clima-
tology and meteorology, and natural history, including
mineralogy, geology, botany, zoology, and agricultural science. While in Europe, he served as a scientific scout,
sharing his observations with others. As secretary of state, he
submitted a report to Congress on weights and measures in
1790. He was the president of the American Philosophical
Society from 1797 to 1814.

I could wish to correspond with you ... of the true power of
our climate as discoverable from the thermometer, from the
force and direction of the winds, the quantity of rain, the plants
which grow without shelter in winter etc. On the other hand, we
should be much pleased with contemporary observations of the
same particulars in your country, which will give us a compara-
tive view of the two climates. Fahrenheit's thermometer is the
only one in use with us. I make my daily observations as early as
possible in the morning and again about 4 o'clock in the
afternoon, these generally showing the maxima of cold and heat
in the course of twenty-four hours. I wish I could gratify your
botanical taste, but I am acquainted with nothing more than the
first principles of that science.
Letter to Giovanni Fabbroni   *June 8, 1778*

Ignorance is preferable to error, and he is less remote from
the truth who believes nothing than he who believes what is
wrong.
Notes on the State of Virginia   *1781–1785*

When your mind shall be well improved with science, nothing will be necessary to place you in the highest points of view but to pressure the interests of your country, the interests of your friends, and your own interests also, with the purest integrity, the most chaste honor; the defect of these virtues can never be made up by all the other acquirement of body and mind. Make these, then, your first object.

Letter to Peter Carr   *August 19, 1785*

It is always better to have no ideas than false ones and to believe nothing than what is wrong. In my mind theories are more easily demolished than rebuilt.

Letter to Rev. James Madison   *July 19, 1788*

What a field have we set at our doors to signalize ourselves in! The botany of America is far from being exhausted, its mineralogy is untouched, and its Natural History or Zoology totally mistaken and misrepresented. ... It is the work to which the young men you are forming should lay their hands. We have spent the prime of our lives in procuring them the precious blessing of liberty. Let them spend theirs in showing that it is the great parent of science and virtue, and that a nation will be great in both always in proportion as it is free.

Letter to Dr. Joseph Willard   *March 24, 1789*

Your favor of October 15. inclosing a drawing of your cotton gin, was received on the 6th. inst. The only requisite of the law now uncomplied with is the forwarding of a model, which, being received, your patent may be made out and delivered to your order immediately. As the state of Virginia, of which I am, carries on household manufactures of cotton to a great extent, as I also do myself, and one of the great embarrassments is the cleaning the cotton of the seed, I feel a considerable interest in the success of your invention for family use.

Letter to Eli Whitney   *November 16, 1793*

I am for encouraging the progress of science in all its branches.

Letter to Elbridge Gerry   *January 26, 1799*

It is impossible for a man who takes a survey of what is already known not to see what an immensity in every branch of science yet remains to be discovered.

Letter to William Green Munford   *June 18, 1799*

The bearer hereof is Mr. Whitney at Connecticut, a mechanic of the first order of ingenuity, who invented the cotton gin now so much used in the south; he is at the head of a considerable gun manufactory in Connecticut, and furnishes the U.S. with muskets, undoubtedly the best they receive. He has invented molds and machines for making all the pieces of his locks so exactly equal that taking 100 locks to pieces and mingle their parts and the hundred locks may be put together as well by taking the first pieces which come to hand.

Letter to James Monroe   *November 14, 1801*

I have received a copy of the evidence at large respecting the discovery of the vaccine inoculation which you have been pleased to send me and for which I return you my thanks. Having been among the early converts in this part of the globe to its efficiency, I took an early part in recommending it to my countrymen.

Letter to Dr. Edward Jenner   *May 14, 1806*

The only sure foundations of medicine are in intimate knowledge of the human body and observation on the effects of medicinal substances on that. The anatomical and clinical schools, therefore, are those in which the young physician should be formed. If he enters with innocence that of the theory of medicine, it is scarcely possible he should come out untainted with error.

Letter to Dr. Caspar Wistar   *June 21, 1807*

Nature intended me for the tranquil pursuits of science by rendering them my supreme delight. But the enormities of the times in which I have lived have forced me to take a part in resisting them, and to commit myself on the boisterous ocean of political passions.

Letter to Pierre Samuel Du Pont de Nemours   *March 2, 1809*

But even in Europe a change has sensibly taken place in the mind of man. Science had liberated the ideas of those who read and reflect, and the American example had kindled feelings of right in the people. An insurrection has consequently begun of science, talents, and courage, against rank and birth, which have fallen into contempt. It has failed in its first effort, because the mobs of the cities, the instrument used for its accomplishment, debased by ignorance, poverty, and vice, could not be restrained to rational action. But the world will recover from the panic of this first catastrophe. Science is progressive, and talents and enterprise on the alert.

Letter to John Adams   *October 28, 1813*

Botany I rank with the most valuable sciences, whether we consider its subjects as furnishing the principal subsistence of life to man and beast, delicious varieties for our tables, refreshments from our orchards, the adornments of our flower borders, shade and perfume of our groves, materials for our buildings, or medicaments for our bodies.

Letter to Dr. Thomas Cooper   *February 10, 1814*

Nature has, in truth, produced units only through all her works. Classes, orders, genera, species are not of her work. Her creation is of individuals. No two animals are exactly alike; no two plants, nor even two leaves or blades of grass; no two crystallizations. And if we may venture from what is within the cognizance of such organs as ours to conclude on that beyond their powers, we must believe that no two particles of matter are of exact resemblance. This infinitude of units or individuals being far beyond the capacity of our memory, we are obliged, in aid of that, to distribute them into masses, throwing into each of these all the individuals which have a certain degree of resemblance; to subdivide these again into smaller groups, according to certain points of dissimilitude observable in them; and so on until we have formed what we call a system of classes, orders, genera, and species.

Letter to Dr. John Manners   *February 22, 1814*

JEFFERSON
ON EDUCATION

*T*homas Jefferson may have been the chief spokesman for public education in the eighteenth and early nineteenth centuries. In his 1785 bill submitted to the Virginia Legislature for the More General Diffusion of Knowledge, he proposed that all free children, male and female, receive free education for three years. He supported further public education in grammar schools. When he retired from the presidency in 1809, he began planning for the University of Virginia, which was chartered in 1819 and opened to students in 1825. Jefferson regarded formal education as the beginning of the process of lifelong learning.

I accordingly prepared three bills for the Revisal, proposing three distinct grades of education, reaching all classes: 1. Elementary schools for all children generally, rich and poor. 2. Colleges for a middle degree of instruction, calculated for the common purposes of life, and such as would be desirable for all who are in easy circumstances. And 3. An ultimate grade for teaching the sciences generally and in their highest degree.

Autobiography   *February 7, 1821*

The reading in the first stage, where they will receive their whole education, is proposed, as has been said, to be chiefly historical. History by appraising them of the past will enable them to judge of the future; it will avail them of the experiences of other times and other nations; it will qualify them as judges of the actions and designs of men; it will enable them to know ambition under every disguise it may assume; and knowing it, to defeat its views.

Notes on the State of Virginia   *1781–1785*

But why send an American youth to Europe for education? What are the objects of an useful American education? Classical knowledge; modern languages, chiefly French, Spanish, and Italian; Mathematics; Natural Philosophy; Natural History; Civil History and Ethics. In Natural Philosophy, I mean to include Chemistry and Agriculture, and in Natural History to include Botany, as well as the other branches of those departments. It is true that the habit of speaking the modern languages cannot be as well acquired in America, but every other article can be as well acquired at William and Mary College as at any other place in Europe.

Letter to John Bannister, Jr.   *October 15, 1785*

Preach, my dear Sir, a crusade against ignorance; establish and improve the law for educating the common people. Let our countrymen know that the people alone can protect us against these evils, and that the tax which will be paid for this purpose is not more than the thousandth part of what will be paid to kings, priests, and nobles which will rise up among us if we leave the people in ignorance.

Letter to George Wythe   *August 13, 1786*

Where are you, my dear Maria? How are you occupied? Write me a letter by the first post, and answer me all these questions. Tell me whether you see the sun rise every day? How many pages you read every day in *Don Quixote?* How far you are advanced in him? Whether you repeat a grammar lesson every day? What else you read? How many hours a day you sew? Whether you have an opportunity of continuing your music? Whether you know how to make a pudding yet, to cut out a beefsteak, to sow spinach? Be good, my dear, as I have always found you; never be angry with anybody nor speak harm of them; try to let everybody's faults be forgotten as you would wish yours to be; take more pleasure in giving what is best to another than in giving it to yourself.

Letter to Mary Jefferson   *April 11, 1790*

Your resolution to apply to the study of the law is wise in my opinion, and at the same time to mix with it a good degree of attention to the farm. The one will relieve the other.

Letter to Thomas Mann Randolph   *May 30, 1790*

We wish to establish in the upper and healthier country, and more centrally for the state, an University on a plan so broad and liberal and modern as to be worth patronizing with the public support, and be a temptation to the youth of other states to come and drink of the cup of knowledge and fraternize with us.

Letter to Dr. Joseph Priestley   *January 18, 1800*

A part of my occupation, and by no means the least pleasing, is the direction of the studies of such young men as ask it. They place themselves in the neighboring village, and have the use of my library and counsel, and make a part of my society. In advising the course of their reading, I endeavor to keep their attention fixed on the main objects of all science, the freedom and happiness of man.

Letter to General Tadeusz Kosciusko   *February 26, 1810*

Our post-revolutionary youths are born under happier stars than you and I were. They acquire all learning in their mother's womb and bring it into the world ready made. The information of books is no longer necessary, and all knowledge which is not innate is in contempt, or neglected at least. Every folly must run its round, and so, I suppose, must that of self-learning and self-sufficiency, of rejecting the knowledge acquired in past ages and starting on the new ground of intuition. When sobered by experience, I hope our successors will turn their attention to the advantages of education—I mean of education on the broad scale.

Letter to John Adams   *July 5, 1814*

Enlighten the people generally, and tyranny and oppression of the body and mind will vanish like evil spirits at the dawn of day.

Letter to Pierre Samuel Du Pont de Nemours   *April 24, 1816*

A system of general instruction, which shall reach every description of our citizens, from the richest to the poorest, as it was the earliest so will it be the latest of all the public concerns in which I shall permit myself to take an interest.

Letter to Joseph C. Cabell   *January 14, 1818*

My surviving daughter accordingly, the mother of many daughters as well as sons, has made their education the object of her life, and being a better judge of the practical part than myself, it is with her aid that I shall subjoin a catalogue of the books for such a course of reading as we have practiced.

Letter to Nathaniel Burwell   *March 14, 1818*

As well might it be urged that the wild and uncultivated tree, hitherto yielding sour and bitter fruit only, can never be made to yield better; yet we know that the grafting art implants a new tree on the savage stock, producing what is most estimable both in kind and degree. Education, in like manner, engrafts a new man on the native stock, and improves what in his nature was vicious and perverse into qualities of virtue and social worth.

Report on University of Virginia   *August 4, 1818*

Among the values of classical learning, I estimate the luxury of reading the Greek and Roman authors in all the beauties of their originals. And why should not this innocent and elegant luxury take its preeminent stand ahead of all those addressed merely to the senses? I think myself more indebted to my father for this than for all the other luxuries his cares and affections have placed within my reach.

Letter to John Brazier   *August 24, 1819*

I do not write with the ease which your letter of September 18. supposes. Crippled wrists and fingers make writing slow and laborious. But while writing to you, I lose the sense of these things in the recollection of ancient times, when youth and health made happiness out of every thing. I forget for a while the hoary winter of old age, when we can think of nothing but how to keep ourselves warm, and how to get rid of our heavy hours until the friendly hand of death shall rid us of all at once. Against this *tedium vitae,* however, I fortunately mounted on a hobby, which indeed I should have better managed some thirty or forty years ago, but whose easy amble is still sufficient to give exercise and amusement to an Octogenary rider. This is the establishment of a University.

Letter to John Adams   *October 12, 1823*

JEFFERSON
ON BOOKS

D*uring his lifetime, Jefferson built three personal libraries. The first was destroyed in a fire in February 1770 at Shadwell. After the British burned Washington in the War of 1812, Jefferson offered his library for sale to the United States on September 21, 1814, and it became the foundation of the Library of Congress. He then rebuilt his book collection during the remaining years of his life.*

My late loss may perhaps have reached you by this time; I mean the loss of my mother's house by fire, and in it of every paper I had in the world, and almost every book. On a reasonable estimate I calculate the cost of the books burned to have been £200 sterling. Would to God it had been the money, then had it never cost me a sigh! To make the loss more sensible, it fell principally on my books of Common Law, of which I have but one left, at that time lent out.

Letter to John Page   *February 21, 1770*

A lively and lasting sense of filial duty is more effectively impressed on the mind of a son or daughter by reading *King Lear* than by all the dry volumes of ethics and divinity that ever were written.

Letter to Robert Skipwith   *August 3, 1771*

An honest heart being the first blessing, a knowing head is the second. It is time for you now to begin to be choice in your reading, to begin to pursue a regular course in it, and not to suffer yourself to be turned to the right or left by reading any thing out of that course.

Letter to Peter Carr   *August 19, 1785*

I advise you to begin a course of ancient history, reading everything in the original and not in translations.

Letter to Peter Carr   *August 19, 1785*

I have at length made up the purchases of books for you, as far as it can be done at present. The objects which I have not yet been able to get I shall continue to seek for. Those purchased are packed this morning in two trunks, and you have the catalogue and prices herein enclosed.

Letter to James Madison   *September 1, 1785*

Books, really good, acquire just reputation in that time, and so become known to us and communicate to us all their advances in knowledge.

Letter to Charles Bellini   *September 30, 1785*

The losses I have sustained by lending my books will be my apology to you for asking your particular attention to the replacing them in the presses as fast as you finish them, and not to lend them to anybody else, nor suffer anybody to have a book out of the study under cover of your name.

Letter to John Garland Jefferson   *June 11, 1790*

I have often thought that nothing would do more extensive good at small expense than the establishment of a small circulating library in every county, to consist of a few well-chosen books, to be lent to the people of the county under such regulations as would secure their safe return in due time. These should be such as would give them a general view of other history and particular view of their own country, a tolerable knowledge of Geography, the elements of Natural Philosophy, of Agriculture and Mechanics.

Letter to John Wyche   *May 19, 1809*

I am really mortified to be told that, in the United States of America, a fact like this can become a subject of inquiry, and of criminal inquiry too, as an offence against religion; that a question about the sale of a book can be carried before the civil magistrate. Is this then our freedom of religion? And are we to have a censor whose imprimatur shall say what books may be sold, and what we may buy? And who is thus to dogmatize religious opinions for our citizens? Whose foot is to be the measure to which ours are all to be cut or stretched?

Letter to Nicholas Gouin Dufief   *April 19, 1814*

I learn from the newspapers that the vandalism of our enemy has triumphed at Washington over science as well as the arts by the destruction of the public library with the noble edifice in which it was deposited. ... I presume it will be among the early objects of Congress to re-commence their collection. This will be difficult while the War continues and intercourse with Europe is attended with so much risk. You know my collection, its condition and extent. I have been fifty years making it and have spared no pains, opportunity, or expense to make it what it is. While residing in Paris, I devoted every afternoon I was disengaged, for a summer or two, in examining all the principal book stores, turning over every book with my own hand and putting by everything which relates to America, and indeed whatever was rare and valuable in every science. Besides this, I had standing orders during the whole time I was in Europe on its principal book marts, particularly Amsterdam, Frankfort, Madrid, and London, for such works relating to America as could not be found in Paris. So that in that department particularly, such a collection was made as probably can never again be effected, because it is hardly probable that the same opportunities, the same time, industry, perseverance, and expense, with some knowledge of the bibliography of the subject, would again happen to be in concurrence. During the same period, and after my return to America, I was led to procure also whatever related to the duties of those in the high concerns of the nation. So that the collection which I suppose is between nine and ten thousand volumes, while it includes what is chiefly valuable in science and literature generally, extends more particularly to whatever belongs to the American statesman. In the diplomatic and parliamentary branches, it is particularly full. It is long since I have been sensible it ought not to continue private property, and had provided that at my death, Congress shall have the refusal of it at their own price. But the loss they have now incurred makes the present the proper moment for their accommodation, without regard to the small remnant of time and the barren use of my enjoying it.

Letter to Samuel Harrison Smith   *September 21, 1814*

You are pleased to ask my opinion on the subject of the arrangement of libraries. I shall communicate with pleasure what occurs to me on it. Two methods offer themselves, the one alphabetical, the other according to the subject of the book. The former is very unsatisfactory, because of the medley it presents to the mind, the difficulty sometimes of recalling the author's name and the greater difficulty, where the name is not given, of selecting the word in the title, which shall determine its alphabetical place. The arrangement according to subject is far preferable, although sometimes presenting difficulty also, for it is often doubtful to which subject a book should be ascribed.

Letter to George Watterston   *May 7, 1815*

I cannot live without books.
Letter to John Adams   *June 10, 1815*

My repugnance to the writing table becomes daily and hourly more deadly and insurmountable. In place of this has come on a canine appetite for reading. And I indulge it because I see in it a relief against the *taedium senectutis* ("weariness of old age"), a lamp to lighten my path through the dreary wilderness of time before me, whose bourne I see not. Losing daily all interest in the things around us, something else is necessary to fill the void. With me it is reading, which occupies the mind without the labor of producing ideas from my own stock.

Letter to John Adams   *May 17, 1818*

I was a hard student until I entered on the business of life, the duties of which leave no idle time to those disposed to fulfill them; and now, retired and at the age of seventy-six, I am again a hard student. Indeed, my fondness for reading and study revolts me from the drudgery of letter writing. ... I never go to bed without an hour's ... reading of something moral.

Letter to Dr. Vine Utley   *March 21, 1819*

JEFFERSON ON
FRIENDS AND FAMILY

O n January 1, 1772, Thomas Jefferson married Martha Wayles Skelton, a twenty-three-year-old widow. She died on September 6, 1782, a few months after the birth of their sixth child. Of the six children, only two, Martha (called Patsy) and Mary (called Maria or Polly), lived to maturity. Many grandchildren lived with him at Monticello. At his death in 1826, Thomas Jefferson had one living child (Martha), eleven living grandchildren, and fourteen great-grandchildren. His family was very important to him. He also treasured his many friends, seeing them whenever he could and writing them often. It is estimated that Jefferson wrote approximately 20,000 letters in his lifetime.

But friendship is precious, not only in the shade but in the sunshine of life, and thanks to a benevolent arrangement of things, the greater part of life is sunshine.
Letter to Maria Cosway   *October 12, 1786*

Dear Brother: The very short period of my life which I have passed unconnected with public business suffices to convince me it is the happiest of all situations, and that no society is so precious as that of one's own family.
Letter to Randolph Jefferson   *January 11, 1789*

My Dear Martha: Having no particular subject for a letter, I find none more soothing to my mind than to indulge itself in expressions of the love I bear you, and the delight with which I recall the various scenes through which we have passed together in our wanderings over the world. These reveries alleviate the toils and inquietudes of my present situation and leave me always impressed with the desire of being at home once more, and of exchanging labor, envy, and malice for ease, domestic occupation, and domestic love and society; where I may once more be happy with you, and dear little Anne, with whom even Socrates might ride on a stick without being ridiculous.

Letter to Martha Jefferson Randolph   *January 15, 1792*

To His Dear Daughter: We had peaches and Indian corn on the 12th. instant. When do they begin with you this year? Can you lay up a good stock of seed-peas for the ensuing summer? We will try this winter to cover our garden with a heavy coat of manure. When earth is rich, it bids defiance to droughts, yields in abundance and of the best quality. I suspect that the insects which have harassed you have been encouraged by the feebleness of your plants, and that has been produced by the lean state of the soil. We will attack them another year with joint efforts. We learn that France has set commissioners to England to treat of peace, and imagine it cannot be unacceptable to the latter in the present state of general bankruptcy and demolition of their manufactures. Upon the whole the affairs of France, notwithstanding their difficulties external and internal, appear solid and safe. Present me to all my neighbors; kiss the little ones for me, and my warmest affections to yourself and Mr. Randolph.

Letter to Martha Jefferson Randolph   *July 21, 1793*

In the meantime I am going to Virginia. I have at length become able to fix that to the beginning of the new year. I am then to be liberated from the hated occupations of politics and to remain in the bosom of my family, my farm, and my books. I have my house to build, my fields to farm, and to watch for the happiness of those who labor for mine. I have one daughter married to a man of science, sense, virtue, and competence in whom indeed I have nothing more to wish. They live with me. If the other shall be as fortunate, in due process of time I shall imagine myself as blessed of the patriarchs. Nothing could then withdraw my thoughts a moment from home but the recollection of my friends abroad.

Letter to Mrs. John Barker Church   *November 27, 1793*

My Dear Maria: I received with pleasure your letter from Varina, and though I ever had a moment's doubt of your love for me, yet it gives me infinite delight to read the expressions of it. Indeed I had often and always read it in your affectionate and attentive conduct towards me. On my part, my love to your sister and yourself knows no bounds, and as I scarcely see any other object in life, so would I quit it with desire whenever my continuance in it shall become useless to you.

> *Letter to Mary Jefferson*   *March 11, 1797*

My Dear Children: I am very happy to find that two of you can write. ... I am happy too that Miss Ellen can now read so readily. If she will make haste and read through all the books I have given her and will let me know when she is through them, I will go and carry her some more. I shall now see whether she wishes to see me as much as she says. I wish to see you all and the more I perceive that you are all advancing in your learning and improving in good dispositions, the more I shall love you and the more everybody will love you. It is a charming thing to be loved by everybody, and the way to obtain it is never to quarrel or be angry with anybody and to tell a story. Do all the kind things you can to your companions; give them everything rather than to yourself. Pity and help any thing you see in distress and learn your books and improve your minds. This will make everybody fond of you and desirous of doing it to you. Go on then my dear children, and, when we meet at Monticello, let me see who has improved the most. I kiss this paper for each of you.

> *Letter to Anne Cary, Thomas Jefferson, and*   *March 2, 1802*
> *Ellen Wayles Randolph*

The affectionate sentiments which you have had the goodness to express in your letter of May 20 towards my dear departed daughter have awakened in me sensibilities natural to the occasion and recalled your kindnesses to her, which I shall remember with gratitude and friendship.

> *Letter to Abigail Adams*   *June 13, 1804*

Friends we have, if we have merited them. Those of our earliest years stand nearest in our affections. Our college friends are the dearest.

> *Letter to John Page*   *June 25, 1804*

I find friendship to be like wine, raw when new; ripened with age, the true old man's milk and restorative cordial.

Letter to Dr. Benjamin Rush   *August 17, 1811*

Good wishes are all an old man has to offer his country or friends.

Letter to Thomas Law   *January 15, 1811*

I brought the enclosed book to this place the last fall, intending to forward it to you, but having a neighbor here who loves to laugh, I lent it to him to read; he lent it to another, and so it went the rounds of the neighborhood and is returned to me at my spring visit to this place. I now forward it, and if it diverts you for an hour or two, I shall be gratified by it. I was myself amused by its humor as much as its object would permit me to be; for this is evidently to deride the Republican branches of our government. I left all well at Monticello, except Benjamin, whose health is very precarious. Lewis is becoming the favorite of all. His vivacity, his intelligence, and his beauty (for the mark on his forehead is disappearing) make him a perfect pet. You will perceive from these senile details of the nursery that I am becoming old. I wish I had no other proofs, but I am weakening very sensibly. I can walk no further than my garden. I ride, however, and in a carriage can come here without fatigue. I fear, however, this will not long be the case.

Letter to Mrs. Elizabeth Trist   *May 10, 1813*

My father's education had been quite neglected, but being of a strong mind, sound judgment, and eager after information, he read much and improved himself, insomuch that he was chosen, with Joshua Fry, Professor of Mathematics in William and Mary College, to continue the boundary line between Virginia and North Carolina which had been begun by Colonel Byrd, and was afterwards employed with the same Mr. Fry to make the first map of Virginia which had ever been made, that of Captain Smith being merely a conjectural sketch.

Autobiography   *January 6–July 21, 1821*

JEFFERSON ON RELIGION
AND RELIGIOUS FREEDOM

The Virginia Statute of Religious Freedom was drawn up by Thomas Jefferson in 1777 and introduced into the General Assembly when Jefferson was governor in 1779. There was a long struggle for its enactment, but it was finally passed by the Virginia Senate on January 16, 1786. The act made religious taxes illegal and allowed for liberty of religious opinion. The separation of church and state and freedom of religion became law for the entire country with the passage of the First Amendment to the Constitution, almost two centuries after the founding of Jamestown.

Our rulers can have authority over such natural rights only as we have submitted to them. The rights of conscience we never submitted, we could never submit. We are answerable for them to our God. The legitimate powers of government extend to such acts only as are injurious to others. But it does me no injury for my neighbor to say there are twenty gods or no god. It neither picks my pocket nor breaks my leg. If it be said, his testimony in a court of Justice cannot be relied on; reject it then and be the stigma on him. Constraint may make him worse by making him a hypocrite, but it will never make him a truer man. It may fix him obstinately in his errors, but will not cure them. Reason and free enquiry are the only effectual agents against error.

Notes on the State of Virginia   *1781–1785*

It is error alone which needs the support of government. Truth can stand by itself. Subject opinion to coercion. Who will you make your inquisitors? Fallible men, men governed by bad passions, by private as well as public reasons. And why subject it to coercion? To produce uniformity. But is uniformity of opinion desirable? No more than of face and stature. Introduce the bed of Procustes then, and as there is danger that the large men may beat the small, making us all of a size by lopping the former and stretching the latter. Difference of opinion is advantageous in religion. The several sects perform the office of a *Censor morum* over each other. Is uniformity attainable? Millions of innocent men, women, and children since the introduction of Christianity have been burnt, tortured, fined, and imprisoned; yet we have not advanced one inch toward uniformity. What has been the effect of coercion? To make one half of the world fools and the other half hypocrites.

Notes on the State of Virginia　　　　　　　*1781–1785*

Be it enacted by the General Assembly that no man be compelled to frequent or support any religious worship, place, or ministry whatsoever, nor shall otherwise suffer on account of his religious opinions or belief; but that all men shall be free to profess, and by argument to maintain, their opinion in matters of religion, and that the same shall in no wise diminish, enlarge, or affect their civil capacities.

Virginia Statute of Religious Freedom　　*January 16, 1786*

I am a Christian, in the only sense he wished anyone to be; sincerely attached to his doctrines, in preference to all others; ascribing to himself every human excellence; and believing he never claimed any other.

Letter to Dr. Benjamin Rush　　　　　*April 21, 1803*

Reading, reflection, and time have convinced me that the interests of society require the observation of those moral precepts only in which all religions agree (for all forbid us to murder, steal, plunder, or bear false witness), and that we should not intermeddle with the particular dogmas in which all religions differ and which are totally unconnected with morality.

Letter to James Fishback　　　　*September 27, 1809*

The law for religious freedom, which made a part of this system, having put down the aristocracy of the clergy, and restored to the citizen the freedom of the mind, and those of entails and descents nurturing an equality of condition among them, this on Education would have raised the mass of the people to the high ground of moral respectability necessary to their own safety and to orderly government.

Letter to John Adams   *October 28, 1813*

Our particular principles of religion are a subject of accountability to our god alone. I enquire after no man's and trouble none with mine; nor is it given to us in this life to know whether yours or mine, our friend's or our foe's, are exactly the right.

Letter to Miles King   *September 26, 1814*

I abuse the priests indeed who have so much abused the pure and holy doctrines of their master and who have laid me under no obligations of reticence as to the tricks of their trade. The genuine system of Jesus and the artificial structures they erected to make him the instrument of wealth, power, and preeminence to themselves are as distinct things in my view as light and darkness.

Letter to Rev. Charles Clay   *January 29, 1815*

I, too, have made a wee little book from the same materials, which I call the Philosophy of Jesus; it is a paradigm of his doctrines, made by cutting the texts out of the book and arranging them on the pages of a blank book in a certain order of time or subject. A more beautiful or precious morsel of ethics I have never seen.

Letter to Charles Thomson   *January 6, 1816*

But I have ever thought religion a concern purely between our god and our consciences, for which we were accountable to him and not to the priests. I never told my own religion nor scrutinised that of another. I never attempted to make a convert nor wished to change another's creed. ... For it is in our lives, and not from our words, that our religion must be read.

Letter to Margaret Bayard Smith   *August 6, 1816*

Say nothing of my religion; it is known to my god and myself alone. Its evidence before the world is to be sought in my life. If that has been honest and dutiful to society, the religion which has regulated it cannot be a bad one. It is singular anxiety which some people have that we should all think alike. Would the world be more beautiful were all our faces alike? Were our tempers, our talents, our tastes, our forms, our wishes, aversions, and pursuits cast exactly in the same mould? If no varieties existed in the animal, vegetable, or mineral creation, but all were strictly uniform, catholic, and orthodox, what a world of physical and moral monotony would it be. These are the absurdities into which those run who usurp the throne of god and dictate to him what he should have done.

Letter to Charles Thomson   *January 29, 1817*

I thank you for the discourse on the consecration of the Synagogue in your city, with which you have been pleased to favor me. I have read it with pleasure and instruction, having learned from it some valuable facts in Jewish history which I did not know before. Your sect by its sufferings has furnished a remarkable proof of the universal spirit of religious intolerance inherent in every sect, disclaimed by all while feeble and practiced by all when in power. Our laws have applied the only antidote to this vice, protecting all on an equal footing. But more remains to be done, for although we are free by the law, we are not so in practice.

Letter to Mordecai Manuel Noah   *May 28, 1818*

If the freedom of religion, guaranteed to us by law in theory, can ever rise in practice under the overbearing inquisition of public opinion, truth will prevail over fanaticism and priests will again be restored to their original purity.

Letter to Jared Sparks   *November 4, 1820*

The movements of the heavenly bodies so exactly held in their course by the balance of centrifugal and centripetal forces, the structure of the earth itself, with its distribution of lands, waters and atmosphere, animal and vegetable bodies, examined in all their minutest particles, insects mere atoms of life, yet as perfectly organised as man or mammoth, the mineral substances, their generation and uses, it is impossible, I say, for the human mind not to believe that there is, in all this, design, cause, and effect up to an ultimate cause, a fabricator of all things from matter and motion, their preserver and regulator while permitted to exist in their present forms and their regenerator into new and other forms.

Letter to John Adams   *April 11, 1823*

LIST OF CORRESPONDENTS

Abigail Adams	writer, wife of John Adams
John Adams	second U.S. president
John Bannister, Jr.	Virginian, met Jefferson in France
Charles Bellini	professor at College of William and Mary
Jacob Bigelow	surgeon
Nathaniel Bowditch	Massachusetts scientist
John Brazier	New England clergyman
Nathaniel Burwell	steward, Virginia Estate
Joseph C. Cabell	Virginia legislator
William Carmichael	chargé d'affaires in Spain
Peter Carr	nephew
Colonel Edward Carrington	Virginia officer
Mrs. John Barker Church	old friend
George Rogers Clark	Continental general, conquered the Northwest
Rev. Charles Clay	minister in Williamsburg
Edward Coles	neighbor, secretary to Madison
John B. Colvin	Maryland newspaper editor
Ellen Randolph Coolidge	granddaughter
Dr. Thomas Cooper	scholar, professor
Maria Cosway	French painter, friend
George Divers	neighbor
Alexander Donald	neighbor
Nicholas Gouin Dufief	book dealer, author
Pierre Samuel Du Pont de Nemours	French friend, settled in America
John Wayles Eppes	son-in-law
Giovanni Fabbroni	Italian author, friend
James Fishback	Kentucky doctor and lawyer
Elbridge Gerry	signer of Declaration of Independence
William Branch Giles	congressman from Virginia
Francis Walker Gilmer	old friend
Dr. George Gilmer	nephew of neighbor, studied at Edinburgh
William Hamilton	horticulturalist from Philadelphia
James Heaton	correspondent
William Charles Jarvis	American consul at Lisbon
John Garland Jefferson	son of Jefferson's cousin
Mary (Maria, Polly) Jefferson	daughter
Randolph Jefferson	brother
Dr. Edward Jenner	physician, discovered vaccination
Miles King	plantation owner in Warwick County, Virginia
Samuel Kercheval	resident of Clarke County, Virginia
General Henry Knox	Continental general

Thomas Jefferson

General Tadeusz Kosciusko	Polish patriot, Continental general
Marquis de Lafayette	French reformer, Continental general
C. P. de Lasteyrie	French horticulturalist
Thomas Law	minister
Henry Lee	Continental colonel, cavalry leader
Captain Meriwether Lewis	leader of Lewis and Clark Expedition
James Madison	fourth U.S. president
Rev. James Madison	clergyman
Dr. John Manners	teacher
James Monroe	fifth U.S. president
William Green Munford	professor (?)
Mordecai Manuel Noah	journalist, New York politician
John Page	companion of youth
Thomas Paine	author of *Common Sense*
Charles Willson Peale	American artist
William Plumer	U.S. senator
Dr. Richard Price	British clergyman
Dr. Joseph Priestley	chemist, discovered oxygen
Anne Cary Randolph	granddaughter
Ellen Wayles Randolph	granddaughter
Martha Jefferson Randolph	daughter
Thomas Mann Randolph	lifelong friend
Thomas Mann Randolph, Jr.	son-in-law
Thomas Jefferson Randolph	grandson, author
Dr. Benjamin Rush	signer of Declaration of Independence
Robert Skipwith	brother-in-law
Margaret Bayard Smith	Washington socialite, author
Samuel Harrison Smith	commissioner of revenue
Thomas Jefferson Smith	son of Samuel Harrison Smith
Jared Sparks	historian
John Taylor	political writer, agriculturalist
Elizabeth Blair Thompson	neighbor
Charles Thomson	secretary to Continental Congress
Mrs. Elizabeth Trist	old friend from Philadelphia
Dr. Vine Utley	doctor
Constantine François de Volney	French traveler and scholar
George Washington	first U.S. president
George Watterston	congressional librarian
Roger Weightman	mayor of Washington, D.C.
Eli Whitney	inventor
Dr. Joseph Willard	president of Harvard University
David Williams	superintendent of U.S. Military Academy
Dr. Caspar Wistar	president of American Philosophical Society
John Wyche	librarian
George Wythe	signer of Declaration of Independence
Colonel Charles Yancey	Virginia legislator

BIBLIOGRAPHY

Jefferson's Writings

The Papers of Thomas Jefferson. Edited by Julian P. Boyd et al. 25 vols. to date.
Princeton: Princeton University Press, 1950–.

The Writings of Thomas Jefferson. Edited by Andrew A. Lipscomb and Albert Ellery
Bergh. 20 vols. Washington, D.C., 1903–1904.

The Writings of Thomas Jefferson. Edited by Paul Leicester Ford. 10 vols. New York:
Putnam, 1892–1899.

Account Books and Memorandum Books. Originals at the Library of Congress, the
Massachusetts Historical Society, the Henry E. Huntington Library, the
New York Public Library and the New York Historical Society.

The Commonplace Book of Thomas Jefferson. Edited by Gilbert Chinard. Baltimore:
John Hopkins Press, 1931.

The Family Letters of Thomas Jefferson. Edited by Edwin A. Betts and James A. Bear,
Jr. Columbia: University of Missouri Press, 1966.

The Garden and Farm Books of Thomas Jefferson. Edited by Robert C. Baron. Golden,
Colo.: Fulcrum Publishing, 1987.

Jefferson's Writings. Edited by Merill D. Peterson. New York: The Library of
America, 1984.

Notes on the State of Virginia. London: John Stockdale, 1787. Edited by William
Peden. Reprint. Chapel Hill: University of North Carolina Press,
1955. *Weather Memorandum Books.* Originals at the Library of Congress and
Massachusetts Historical Society.

Books about Jefferson

Adams, William Howard. *Jefferson's Monticello.* New York: Abbeville Press, 1983.

Bear, James A., Jr. *Jefferson at Monticello.* Charlottesville: Thomas Jefferson
Memorial Foundation, 1962.

Bedini, Silvio A. *Thomas Jefferson: Statesman of Science.* New York: Macmillan, 1990.

Betts, Edwin Morris, and Perkins, Hazelhurst Bolton. *Thomas Jefferson's Flower
Garden at Monticello.* Richmond, 1941. Reprint. Charlottesville: University
Press of Virginia, 1986.

Boorstin, Daniel J. *The Lost World of Thomas Jefferson.* New York: Holt, 1948.

Bush, Alfred L. *Life Portraits of Thomas Jefferson.* Charlottesville: Thomas Jefferson
Memorial Foundation, 1962.

Conant, James B. *Thomas Jefferson and the Development of American Public Education.*
Berkeley: University of California Press, 1962.

Cunningham, Noble E., Jr. *In Pursuit of Reason*. Baton Rouge: Louisiana State University Press, 1987.

Edwards, Everett E. *Jefferson and Agriculture*. Agricultural History Series, no. 7. Washington: U.S. Department of Agriculture, 1943.

Gilreath, James, and Wilson, Douglas L. *Thomas Jefferson's Library*. Washington: Library of Congress, 1989.

Hatch, Peter J. *The Gardens of Monticello*. Charlottesville: Thomas Jefferson Memorial Foundation, 1992.

Honeywell, Roy J. *The Educational Work of Thomas Jefferson*. Cambridge: Harvard University Press, 1931.

Jackson, Donald. *Thomas Jefferson and the Stony Mountains*. Urbana: University of Illinois Press, 1981.

———. *A Year at Monticello—1795*. Golden, Colo.: Fulcrum Publishing, 1989.

Kimball, Marie. *Thomas Jefferson's Cook Book*. Charlottesville: University Press of Virginia, 1949.

Lehman, Karl. *Thomas Jefferson: American Humanist*. Chicago: University of Chicago Press, 1965.

Malone, Dumas. *Jefferson and His Time*. 6 vols. Boston: Little, Brown, 1948–1981.

Miller, Charles A. *Jefferson and Nature*. Baltimore: John Hopkins University Press, 1988.

Miller, John Chester. *The Wolf by the Ears: Thomas Jefferson and Slavery*. New York: Free Press, 1977.

Nichols, Frederick Doveton. *Thomas Jefferson's Architectural Drawings*. Boston: Massachusetts Historical Society and Charlottesville: Thomas Jefferson Memorial Foundation, 1961.

Nichols, Frederick Doveton, and Bear, James A., Jr. *Monticello: A Guidebook*. Charlottesville: University Press of Virginia, 1967.

Nichols, Frederick Doveton, and Griswold, Ralph E. *Thomas Jefferson Landscape Architect*. Charlottesville: University Press of Virginia, 1978.

Peterson, Merill D. *The Jefferson Image in the American Mind*. New York: Oxford University Press, 1960.

———. *Thomas Jefferson and the New Nation*. New York: Oxford University Press, 1970.

Randolph, Sarah N. *The Domestic Life of Thomas Jefferson*. New York: Harper, 1871. Reprint. Charlottesville: Thomas Jefferson Memorial Foundation, 1934.

Sanford, Charles. *The Religious Life of Thomas Jefferson*. Charlottesville: University Press of Virginia, 1984.

Wills, Garry. *Inventing America—Jefferson's Declaration of Independence*. New York: Doubleday, 1978.